Solving Word Problems for Life,
Grades 3–5

Melony A. Brown

Teacher Ideas Press, an imprint of Libraries Unlimited
Westport, Connecticut • London

Library of Congress Cataloging-in-Publication Data

Brown, Melony A.
    Solving word problems for life, grades 3-5 / by Melony A. Brown.
      p. cm.
    Includes index.
    ISBN: 1–59469–011–1 (pbk. : alk. paper)
    1. Arithmetic—Study and teaching (Elementary) 2. word problems
(Mathematics) I. Title.
QA115.B845   2005
372.7—dc22   2005047481

British Library Cataloguing in Publication Data is available.

First published in 2005

Libraries Unlimited/Teacher Ideas Press, 88 Post Road West, Westport, CT 06881
A Member of the Greenwood Publishing Group, Inc.
www.lu.com

Printed in the United States of America

The paper used in this book complies with the
Permanent Paper Standard issued by the National
Information Standards Organization (Z39.48–1984).

10 9 8 7 6 5 4 3 2 1

Contents

Letter to the Teacher

Dear Educator,

You have selected an excellent tool to obtain large growths in your students' math calculation and math reasoning skills! The prep time is minimal because this book is laid out with you in mind.

- Each page has two word problems on it—photocopy each page and then cut the paper into two halves. This will give you two days' worth of warm-up problems ready for use. The students can store the word problems in pencil pouches that can be kept in a three-ring binder notebook.

- The first six daily word problems teach the six basic math skills by introducing the students to visual cues that will be used throughout the book. For a student with learning issues, visual cues are valuable tools in remembering how to complete the steps of a process. The reproducible Visual Cue Card can be photocopied on bright colored paper and laminated to keep in their notebooks to refer back to throughout the year to help them remember the visual cues. You, as the teacher, will need to reinforce the visual cues as you go over the answers to each word problem with your students. Reinforcement is the key to growth in attaining these skills.

- The math skills needed for each problem are identified by the visual cue(s) below the word problem. These visual cues guide the student into the necessary steps needed to solve the problem.

- Use the word problems as a daily warm-up activity in which the students work on the problem independently. There are 180 daily word problems in this book—one for each day of the school year. As the teacher, you will need to monitor their work by initialing it (or they will wait for you to go over it—thus never trying it for themselves!).

- Give the students about seven to ten minutes to work on the problem. The problems are not intended to take any longer than this. If they need longer than ten minutes, the student is not working—he or she is confused about what the problem is asking or is not focused on the task yet.

- At the end of each warm-up period, the teacher should ask if any of the students think they have solved the problem. Have the students explain how they solved the problem, not just give the answer. The process is far more important than just the answer. The process of working the problem is where most students get lost. If they don't get the right answer, but only hear the answer given, they give up. Spend the time explaining how to arrive at the correct answer.

- Each unit comprises fifteen days' worth of problems. Each unit is a mixture of the six basic math skills plus a few extra fun ones from time to time. It ends with a five-question quiz on the sixteenth day. The quiz is composed of five word problems from the previous fifteen days; however, the student has to complete the word problems independently (not waiting on the teacher or neighboring student to go over the answers).

- Each unit (fifteen word problems) should be taken up on quiz day for a notebook or participation grade to keep the students involved in the learning process. To make it easier to keep up with the half sheets of paper, the pencil pouches (mentioned before) can be purchased and placed in a three-ring binder. The word problems are numbered sequentially, so it should be easy to keep them in order when students are asked to turn them in on quiz day!

- Hard Hat Thinking—Extra Credit: These are more involved problems that challenge those students who want to go beyond the problems worked on in class. There are five pages with five problems each at the end of the book. They can be given for extra credit at any time during the year. One caution: Once a grade is given to the student, do not return the sheet to him or her because it might find its way into the hands of another student who might copy the answers and turn it in for his or her extra credit grade.

Enjoy this learning tool with the students. It is on their level—the problems are intended to relate to their life experiences. Reinforce the concepts during the math lessons you teach during class. Watch with amazement how each student's math skills increase!

NCTM Standards

Solving Word Problems for Life, Grades 3–5 is correlated to the following NCTM standards:

- Develop fluency in adding, subtracting, multiplying, and dividing

- Understand the effects of multiplying and dividing whole numbers

- Recognize and generate equivalent forms of commonly used fractions, decimals, and percents

- Develop and use strategies to estimate computations involving fractions and decimals in situations relevant to students' experiences

- Use visual models and equivalent forms to add and subtract commonly used fractions and decimals

- Select and apply appropriate standard units and tools to measure length, area, volume, weight, time, and temperature

- Develop strategies to determine the surface area and volumes of rectangular solids

- Build new mathematical knowledge through problem solving

- Solve problems that arise in mathematics and in other contexts

- Monitor and reflect on the process of mathematical problem solving

- Communicate their mathematical thinking coherently and clearly to peers, teachers, and others

- Create and use representations to organize, record, and communicate mathematical ideas

Reproducible Visual Cue Card

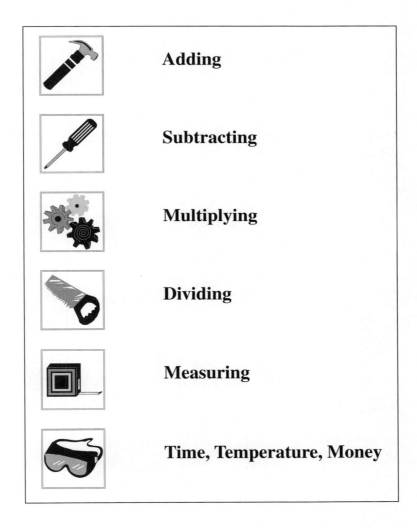

Adding

Subtracting

Multiplying

Dividing

Measuring

Time, Temperature, Money

Unit 1

Day 1–Day 16

SOLVING WORD PROBLEMS FOR LIFE
Day 2

Name _____ Date _____

Link your thinking to tools. The visual cues will help you remember what steps to take!

SUBTRACTING

When you use a screwdriver to take out a screw, you are subtracting or removing it. Therefore, the visual picture of a screwdriver should trigger your mind to subtract.

Example:

The amusement park was 25 miles from Jacob's house. After driving 16 miles, his dad stopped at the gas station. How many more miles is it to the amusement park?

25 miles to the amusement park − 16 miles to the gas station = 9 more miles to the amusement park

---

SOLVING WORD PROBLEMS FOR LIFE
Day 1

Name _____ Date _____

How do I solve word problems, anyway? Easy . . . link your thinking to tools. The visual cues will help you remember what steps to take!

ADDING

When you use a hammer and nails, you are adding to an existing project. Therefore, the visual picture of a hammer should trigger your mind to add.

Example:

Michelle and Tracy had a garage sale. Michelle earned $213 from her sales. Tracy earned $188 from her sales. How much money did they make altogether at the garage sale?

$213 (Michelle's sales) + $188 (Tracy's sales) = $410 total

SOLVING WORD PROBLEMS FOR LIFE
Day 3

Name _____ Date _____

Link your thinking to tools. The visual cues will help you remember what steps to take!

MULTIPLYING

When you use gears, you are multiplying your efforts in moving something. Therefore, the visual picture of gears should trigger your mind to multiply.

Example:

Alexander counted the number of friends at his birthday party. There were 9 kids, and each one was given 3 water balloons to throw at the clown. How many water balloons were there?

9 kids × 3 water balloons each = 27 water balloons

SOLVING WORD PROBLEMS FOR LIFE
Day 4

Name _____ Date _____

Link your thinking to tools. The visual cues will help you remember what steps to take!

DIVIDING

When you use a saw, you are cutting (or dividing) the wood into pieces. Therefore, the visual picture of a saw should trigger your mind to divide.

Example:

Ellen's mom ordered 3 pizzas that had 18 pieces total. If there were 9 girls at her house for dinner, how many pieces of pizza did each girl eat?

18 pieces of pizza ÷ 9 girls = 2 pieces of pizza each

3

SOLVING WORD PROBLEMS FOR LIFE
Day 5

Name _____ Date _____

Link your thinking to tools. The visual cues will help you remember what steps to take!

MEASURING

When you use a tape measure, you are measuring the distance or length of something. Therefore, the visual picture of a tape measure should trigger your mind to measure.

Example:

The road race course was a rectangle. It was 20 blocks long and 8 blocks wide. What is the distance of the road race course?

Hint: Perimeter = length + length + width + width

20 blocks + 20 blocks + 8 blocks + 8 blocks = 56 blocks

SOLVING WORD PROBLEMS FOR LIFE
Day 6

Name _____ Date _____

Link your thinking to tools. The visual cues will help you remember what steps to take!

TIME, TEMPERATURE, AND MONEY

Time, temperature, and money are used all the time. Knowing how and why to use goggles is important for the safe and smart use of tools. Knowing how and why time, temperature, and money are used is important for you because they are used everyday. Therefore, the visual picture of goggles should trigger your mind to time, temperature, and money.

Example:

Joel had 8 dimes and 3 nickels. Dan had 3 quarters and 5 nickels. Who had more money?

Joel: 10¢ + 10¢ + 10¢ + 10¢ + 10¢ + 10¢ + 10¢ + 10¢ + 5¢ + 5¢ + 5¢ = 95¢

Dan: 25¢ + 25¢ + 25¢ + 5¢ + 5¢ + 5¢ + 5¢ + 5¢ = $1.00

SOLVING WORD PROBLEMS FOR LIFE
Day 8

Name _____ Date _____

Mary Beth walked her dog around the block in her neighborhood. The 2 long sides (length) were 25 yards each. The 2 short sides (width) were 14 yards each. What is the total distance (perimeter) around the block?

HOW DO YOU SOLVE IT?

SOLVING WORD PROBLEMS FOR LIFE
Day 7

Name _____ Date _____

Tim had 8 letters to mail to his pen pals. Each letter needed 3 stamps. How many stamps did he need to buy?

HOW DO YOU SOLVE IT?

SOLVING WORD PROBLEMS FOR LIFE
Day 9

Name _____ Date _____

Ms. Johnson's class went to recess at 12:30 P.M. They went back to the classroom at 12:50 P.M. How long was recess?

HOW DO YOU SOLVE IT?

SOLVING WORD PROBLEMS FOR LIFE
Day 10

Name _____ Date _____

In July, there were 20 sunny days, 9 rainy days, and 2 partly cloudy days. How many more sunny days were there than rainy days?

HOW DO YOU SOLVE IT?

SOLVING WORD PROBLEMS FOR LIFE
Day 11

Name _____ Date _____

Frank's ice cream shop sold 69 single-scoop cones and 54 double-scoop cones today. How many cones were sold altogether?

HOW DO YOU SOLVE IT?

SOLVING WORD PROBLEMS FOR LIFE
Day 12

Name _____ Date _____

Darren's allowance is $5.00 per week. He decided to buy a toy army truck for $3.12. How much change will he get back if he spends all of his allowance?

HOW DO YOU SOLVE IT?

SOLVING WORD PROBLEMS FOR LIFE
Day 13

Name _____ Date _____

Sarah planted tulips in her yard. She planted 4 rows with 6 tulips in each row. How many tulips did she plant?

HOW DO YOU SOLVE IT?

SOLVING WORD PROBLEMS FOR LIFE
Day 14

Name _____ Date _____

It was 43°F when Conner woke up, but by 3:00 P.M. it was 76°F. How much had the temperature risen during the day?

HOW DO YOU SOLVE IT?

SOLVING WORD PROBLEMS FOR LIFE
Day 15

Name _____ Date _____

Jake had a marble collection. He had 39 tiger eyes, 26 jaspers, and 10 chinas. How many marbles does he have altogether?

HOW DO YOU SOLVE IT?

SOLVING WORD PROBLEMS FOR LIFE
Day 16—Quiz 1

Name _____ Date _____

Solve the following word problems. Show your work!

1. Derrick used his $5.00 allowance to buy a toy army truck. How much change did he get back if it costs $3.12?

2. Tim mailed 8 letters to his pen pals. If each letter needed 3 stamps, how many stamps did he need to buy?

3. What is the visual cue for subtracting?

4. Frank's ice cream shop sold 69 single-scoop cones and 54 double-scoop cones. How many cones did he sell altogether?

5. Ms. Johnson's class went to recess at 12:30 P.M. They went back to the classroom at 12:50 P.M. How long was recess?

Unit 2

Day 17–Day 32

SOLVING WORD PROBLEMS FOR LIFE
Day 17

Name _____ Date _____

For her birthday, Jenna was given a box of 64 crayons and a coloring book. She lost 18 crayons. How many does she have left?

HOW DO YOU SOLVE IT?

SOLVING WORD PROBLEMS FOR LIFE
Day 18

Name _____ Date _____

For a class project, Ethan had to count the number of vehicles parked at the mall. He counted 516 cars, 104 trucks, 791 SUVs, and 28 motorcycles. How many vehicles were parked at the mall?

HOW DO YOU SOLVE IT?

SOLVING WORD PROBLEMS FOR LIFE
Day 19

Name _____ Date _____

Yvette bought 3 balloons for $1.57. How much change would she get back if she gave the clerk $2.00? How many dimes and pennies would that be?

HOW DO YOU SOLVE IT?

SOLVING WORD PROBLEMS FOR LIFE
Day 20

Name _____ Date _____

Tina's art project used a 9-inch-long by 9-inch-wide frame. How much area did her picture cover?

HOW DO YOU SOLVE IT?

SOLVING WORD PROBLEMS FOR LIFE
Day 21

Name _____ Date _____

Jason left his house at 10:17 A.M. to ride his bike to Jeremy's house. He arrived at his house at 10:33 A.M. How long did it take to ride to Jeremy's house?

HOW DO YOU SOLVE IT?

SOLVING WORD PROBLEMS FOR LIFE
Day 22

Name _____ Date _____

Chandler and Mike had a pizza-eating contest. Chandler ate 6 of the 8 pieces of his pizza. Mike ate 3 of the 4 pieces of his pizza. Who ate more?

HOW DO YOU SOLVE IT?

Draw a picture to solve:

SOLVING WORD PROBLEMS FOR LIFE
Day 23

Name _____ Date _____

The girls' swim team swam laps during practice to train for the swim meet. If 6 girls each swam 7 laps, how many laps did they swim altogether?

HOW DO YOU SOLVE IT?

SOLVING WORD PROBLEMS FOR LIFE
Day 24

Name _____ Date _____

Chef Robert at the Grande Hotel prepared 103 breakfasts, 347 lunches, and 459 dinners. How many meals did he prepare that day?

HOW DO YOU SOLVE IT?

SOLVING WORD PROBLEMS FOR LIFE
Day 25

Name _____ Date _____

Kurt wanted to see how much he had grown during the school year. If he was 3'11" at the beginning of the year and 4'4" at the end of the year, how much had he grown?

HOW DO YOU SOLVE IT?

SOLVING WORD PROBLEMS FOR LIFE
Day 26

Name _____ Date _____

Stephan sold 7 cups of lemonade for 5¢ a cup to a group of kids. If one of the kids gave him 2 quarters, how much change did he give back?

HOW DO YOU SOLVE IT?

SOLVING WORD PROBLEMS FOR LIFE
Day 27

Name _____ Date _____

Troop leader Ken woke us up so early! We went to sleep at 11:00 P.M., and he woke us up at 6:00 A.M. How much sleep did the campers get?

HOW DO YOU SOLVE IT?

SOLVING WORD PROBLEMS FOR LIFE
Day 28

Name _____ Date _____

Mr. Baker assigned 25 problems for homework twice this week. He also assigned 10 problems for extra credit. How many problems did Mr. Baker assign this week?

HOW DO YOU SOLVE IT?

SOLVING WORD PROBLEMS FOR LIFE
Day 29

Name _____ Date _____

Farmer Sam had 27 pigs. 13 pigs played in the mud. 5 pigs ate lunch in the yard. How many pigs were left in the barn?

HOW DO YOU SOLVE IT?

SOLVING WORD PROBLEMS FOR LIFE
Day 30

Name _____ Date _____

Nick broke his arm during his baseball game. The doctor said that he would have to wear his cast for 7 weeks. How many days will Nick have to wear his cast?

HOW DO YOU SOLVE IT?

SOLVING WORD PROBLEMS FOR LIFE
Day 31

Name _____ Date _____

A group of girls started a new fad. 3 girls received a slimy frog toy as a gift. Each of those girls gave 2 more girls a slimy frog toy. How many girls had the new fad toy?

HOW DO YOU SOLVE IT?

Draw a chart to solve:

SOLVING WORD PROBLEMS FOR LIFE
Day 32—Quiz 2

Name _____ Date _____

Solve the following word problems. Show your work!

1. Why is the visual cue for measuring the tape measure?

2. During swim practice, 6 girls on the swim team swam 7 laps each. How many laps did they swim altogether?

3. Farmer Sam had 27 pigs. 13 played in the mud, and 5 ate lunch in the yard. How many were left in the barn?

4. Yvette bought 3 balloons for $1.57. How much change did she get back if she gave the clerk $2.00?

5. Chef Robert at the Grande Hotel prepared 103 breakfasts, 347 lunches, and 459 dinners. How many meals did he prepare that day?

Unit 3

Day 33–Day 48

SOLVING WORD PROBLEMS FOR LIFE
Day 33

Name _____ Date _____

It costs $8 to rent jet skis for an hour. Irving has a $5 bill, 10 quarters, and 6 nickels in his piggy bank. Does he have enough money to rent the skis?

HOW DO YOU SOLVE IT?

SOLVING WORD PROBLEMS FOR LIFE
Day 34

Name _____ Date _____

Mr. Jennings picks up a group of 17 kids at one stop, 9 kids at the next stop, and 22 kids at the last stop. How many kids ride Mr. Jennings' bus?

HOW DO YOU SOLVE IT?

SOLVING WORD PROBLEMS FOR LIFE
Day 35

Name _____ Date _____

Aimee wants to buy a summer pass to the amusement park and water park for $135. She has only saved $58. How much more money does she need to save?

HOW DO YOU SOLVE IT?

SOLVING WORD PROBLEMS FOR LIFE
Day 36

Name _____ Date _____

Rebecca babysat her brother while her mom went to the grocery store. Her mom left at 5:05 P.M. and returned at 6:23 P.M. How long was her mom gone shopping?

HOW DO YOU SOLVE IT?

SOLVING WORD PROBLEMS FOR LIFE
Day 37

Name _____ Date _____

A fire assembly was held in the cafeteria. Ms. Wallace's class sat at 4 tables with 5 students at each table. How many students are in Ms. Wallace's class?

HOW DO YOU SOLVE IT?

SOLVING WORD PROBLEMS FOR LIFE
Day 38

Name _____ Date _____

When Ansley bought her mom's coffee, it was 152°F. But her mom forgot about it for a couple of hours. When she drank it, it had chilled to a room temperature of 68°F. How much heat had her coffee lost?

HOW DO YOU SOLVE IT?

SOLVING WORD PROBLEMS FOR LIFE
Day 39

Name _____ Date _____

A passenger train sold 565 tickets. At the first stop, 379 passengers got off the train. How many passengers were left on the train?

HOW DO YOU SOLVE IT?

SOLVING WORD PROBLEMS FOR LIFE
Day 40

Name _____ Date _____

Brady took 540 aluminum cans, 173 plastic bottles, and 388 milk jugs to the recycling center. How many items did he take to the recycling center?

HOW DO YOU SOLVE IT?

25

SOLVING WORD PROBLEMS FOR LIFE
Day 42

Name _____ Date _____

An octopus has 8 tentacles. A scuba diver saw 7 octopi during his diving trip. How many octopus tentacles did he see?

HOW DO YOU SOLVE IT?

SOLVING WORD PROBLEMS FOR LIFE
Day 41

Name _____ Date _____

Tansy wanted to buy a teddy bear for $4.50 and a card for $1.25. How much change did she get back from $10.00 if the tax was 29¢?

HOW DO YOU SOLVE IT?

26

SOLVING WORD PROBLEMS FOR LIFE
Day 43

Name _____ Date _____

The road race course was rectangular in shape—2.5 miles on the long sides and 0.6 miles on the short sides. What was the distance around the course?

Hint: Perimeter = 2(L) + 2(W)

HOW DO YOU SOLVE IT?

SOLVING WORD PROBLEMS FOR LIFE
Day 44

Name _____ Date _____

Allen's family drove to their beach house. They left at 7:30 A.M. They stopped after driving 4 hours and 18 minutes. It took another 2 hours and 12 minutes to get to the beach house. What time did they arrive there?

HOW DO YOU SOLVE IT?

SOLVING WORD PROBLEMS FOR LIFE
Day 45

Name _____ Date _____

Mary said that her brother, Max, is 3 decades plus 6 years old. How old is Max?

HOW DO YOU SOLVE IT?

SOLVING WORD PROBLEMS FOR LIFE
Day 46

Name _____ Date _____

2 kids in the 3rd grade got chicken pox. Those 2 kids each gave it to 2 more kids. Those kids each gave it to 2 more kids. How many kids got the chicken pox?

HOW DO YOU SOLVE IT?

Draw a chart to solve:

SOLVING WORD PROBLEMS FOR LIFE
Day 47

Name _____ Date _____

Toby weighed 320 pounds at the beginning of his diet. During the first 4 months, he lost an average of 17 pounds per month. He lost 8 pounds the 5th month. The last month of his program, he lost 6 pounds. How much weight did he lose?

HOW DO YOU SOLVE IT?

SOLVING WORD PROBLEMS FOR LIFE
Day 48—Quiz 3

Name _____ Date _____

Solve the following word problems. Show your work!

1. A fire safety program was held in the cafeteria. Ms. Wallace's class sat at 4 tables with 5 students each. How many students are in Ms. Wallace's class?

2. Mr. Jennings picks up 17 kids at the first stop, 9 kids at the next stop, and 22 at the last stop. How many kids are on his bus?

3. A passenger train sold 565 tickets. If 379 passengers got off at the first stop, how many passengers were left?

4. What is the perimeter of a race course if it is 2.5 miles in length and 0.6 miles in width?

5. Why is the visual cue for time, temperature, and money a pair of safety goggles?

29

Unit 4

Day 49–Day 64

SOLVING WORD PROBLEMS FOR LIFE
Day 49

Name _____ Date _____

Luke sold 73 boxes of doughnuts for a fundraiser. How many doughnuts did he sell if there are a dozen doughnuts in each box?

HOW DO YOU SOLVE IT?

SOLVING WORD PROBLEMS FOR LIFE
Day 50

Name _____ Date _____

Mallory was paid $16.50 on Friday night and $35.75 on Saturday night for babysitting. How much money did she make babysitting?

HOW DO YOU SOLVE IT?

32

SOLVING WORD PROBLEMS FOR LIFE
Day 51

Name _____ Date _____

There are 720 gumballs in the gumball machine. One-eighth of them are red, one-half are yellow, one-fourth are blue, and one-eighth are green. How many gumballs of each color are there?

HOW DO YOU SOLVE IT?

Write the correct fractions and reduce them to the lowest terms.

SOLVING WORD PROBLEMS FOR LIFE
Day 52

Name _____ Date _____

There are 81 butterflies in the Butterfly House. If there are 9 different types of butterflies, how many of each type of butterfly are in the Butterfly House?

HOW DO YOU SOLVE IT?

33

SOLVING WORD PROBLEMS FOR LIFE
Day 53

Name _____ Date _____

Ellis' teacher was given 9,000 pieces of construction paper at the beginning of the school year. If she had used 6,395 pieces by February, how many pieces did they have left?

HOW DO YOU SOLVE IT?

SOLVING WORD PROBLEMS FOR LIFE
Day 54

Name _____ Date _____

Andrea's mom saw the times she spent talking long distance to her friends. The calls lasted 23 minutes, 11 seconds; 14 minutes, 57 seconds; and 9 minutes, 31 seconds. How long did she talk on the phone?

Hint: 60 seconds = 1 minute

HOW DO YOU SOLVE IT?

SOLVING WORD PROBLEMS FOR LIFE
Day 55

Name _____ Date _____

Evan built a wall around his sand castle. It was 24 inches wide by 40 inches long. How much area did his wall protect?

HOW DO YOU SOLVE IT?

SOLVING WORD PROBLEMS FOR LIFE
Day 56

Name _____ Date _____

Patricia had 8 packs of gum with 15 pieces in each pack. How many pieces of gum did she have?

HOW DO YOU SOLVE IT?

35

SOLVING WORD PROBLEMS FOR LIFE
Day 57

Name _____ Date _____

There are 12 orange, 6 green, 12 yellow, 10 red, and 20 blue water balloons in the bucket. What is the chance of picking up each of the colors?

HOW DO YOU SOLVE IT?

Set each color up as a fraction and reduce them to the lowest terms.

SOLVING WORD PROBLEMS FOR LIFE
Day 58

Name _____ Date _____

Kale bought a pair of sunglasses for $9.24. What coins would he get back from a $10.00 bill if the clerk gave him 4 coins?

HOW DO YOU SOLVE IT?

SOLVING WORD PROBLEMS FOR LIFE
Day 59

Name _____ Date _____

Zookeeper Eddie takes care of 6 zebras, 9 elephants, 13 lions, 12 pandas, 7 giraffes, 5 tigers, 10 gorillas, and 4 rhinoceroses. How many animals is he responsible for?

HOW DO YOU SOLVE IT?

SOLVING WORD PROBLEMS FOR LIFE
Day 60

Name _____ Date _____

Jane's parents needed to know how many tables to decorate for her party. If 65 kids were invited, how many tables would be needed if 8 people can sit at a table?

HOW DO YOU SOLVE IT?

SOLVING WORD PROBLEMS FOR LIFE
Day 61

Name _____ Date _____

Danny had $75.00 to spend at the water park. His ticket was $39.99. Lunch costs $18.68, and the souvenir he wanted costs $23.00. How much money was he short of buying the souvenir?

HOW DO YOU SOLVE IT?

SOLVING WORD PROBLEMS FOR LIFE
Day 62

Name _____ Date _____

John saw this question on his test: "Which one is longer—42 inches or 4 feet?" What should his answer be?

HOW DO YOU SOLVE IT?

38

SOLVING WORD PROBLEMS FOR LIFE
Day 63

Name _____ Date _____

Jill's parents wanted to camp for 3 days. She didn't like camping; she wanted to go home! How many hours before she could go home?

HOW DO YOU SOLVE IT?

SOLVING WORD PROBLEMS FOR LIFE
Day 64—Quiz 4

Name _____ Date _____

Solve the following word problems. Show your work!

1. Why is the visual cue for adding the hammer?

2. How much money did Mallory make from babysitting if she earned $16.50 on Friday night and $35.75 on Saturday night?

3. 65 kids were invited to Jane's party. If 8 kids could sit at a table, how many tables did they need to decorate?

4. How many doughnuts did Luke sell if he sold 73 boxes with a dozen doughnuts in each box?

5. Evan's sand castle had a wall around it protecting it. It was 24 inches wide and 40 inches long. How much area did his wall protect?

Unit 5

Day 65–Day 80

SOLVING WORD PROBLEMS FOR LIFE
Day 65

Name _____ Date _____

Nurse Catherine took Timothy's temperature. It was 103.7°F. How much above normal was it?

HOW DO YOU SOLVE IT?

SOLVING WORD PROBLEMS FOR LIFE
Day 66

Name _____ Date _____

Sarah's teacher assigned the class this homework assignment: Add together all the even numbers up to the number 75. What would her answer be?

HOW DO YOU SOLVE IT?

SOLVING WORD PROBLEMS FOR LIFE
Day 67

Name _____ Date _____

The landscaping crew planted tulips in front of the apartment complex. They planted 8 rows with 25 tulips in each row. How many tulips were planted?

HOW DO YOU SOLVE IT?

SOLVING WORD PROBLEMS FOR LIFE
Day 68

Name _____ Date _____

Thomas' fish aquarium measures 10 inches long, 4 inches wide, and 6 inches high. What is the volume of his aquarium?

HOW DO YOU SOLVE IT?

SOLVING WORD PROBLEMS FOR LIFE
Day 69

Name _____ Date _____

Antonio bought a shirt for $25.99, jeans for $42.50, and a belt for $18.00. How much money did he spend?

HOW DO YOU SOLVE IT?

SOLVING WORD PROBLEMS FOR LIFE
Day 70

Name _____ Date _____

LaTonya wanted to double this cookie recipe for the party: 1 egg, 1/2 c. oil, 1/2 c. sugar, 1 c. flour, 1/4 tsp. baking soda, 1/8 tsp. salt, 1/4 tsp. cinnamon, 1/4 tsp. nutmeg, and 1 3/4 c. oatmeal How much of each ingredient does she need?

HOW DO YOU SOLVE IT?

SOLVING WORD PROBLEMS FOR LIFE
Day 71

Name _____ Date _____

Eddie was born in 1998. If it is his birthday in the year 2020, how old is he?

HOW DO YOU SOLVE IT?

SOLVING WORD PROBLEMS FOR LIFE
Day 72

Name _____ Date _____

Trent's job at the grocery store was to restock shelves. He had 1,500 boxes of cereal to shelve on 5 shelves. How many boxes were placed on each shelf?

HOW DO YOU SOLVE IT?

SOLVING WORD PROBLEMS FOR LIFE
Day 73

Name _____ Date _____

There are 6 plastic snakes, 3 rings, 8 books, 5 pencils, and 2 furry animals in the treasure chest. What are the chances for each item to be picked?

HOW DO YOU SOLVE IT?

Set up each toy as a fraction and reduce them to the lowest terms.

SOLVING WORD PROBLEMS FOR LIFE
Day 74

Name _____ Date _____

Ian was allowed to watch 30 minutes of television per day during the school week and 1 hour a day on the weekends. How many hours of television time does he get each week?

HOW DO YOU SOLVE IT?

SOLVING WORD PROBLEMS FOR LIFE
Day 75

Name _____ Date _____

For the dance at school, each 4th grader is to bring one half-dozen cupcakes. If there are 152 students in the 4th grade, how many cupcakes would that be?

HOW DO YOU SOLVE IT?

SOLVING WORD PROBLEMS FOR LIFE
Day 76

Name _____ Date _____

How many calories did Josh consume if he ate a biscuit with sausage and egg (529 calories), a raspberry Danish (414 calories), and a glass of milk (125 calories)?

HOW DO YOU SOLVE IT?

SOLVING WORD PROBLEMS FOR LIFE
Day 77

Name _____ Date _____

If there are 2 cups in a pint and 8 pints in a gallon, how many cups are there in a gallon? How many cups would be in 4 gallons of milk?

HOW DO YOU SOLVE IT?

SOLVING WORD PROBLEMS FOR LIFE
Day 78

Name _____ Date _____

Holly's grandparents gave the 3 grandkids $300 combined. Holly was given one-half of the money, Matthew was given one-sixth of the money, and Deirdre was given one-third of the money. How much money did each grandkid receive?

HOW DO YOU SOLVE IT?

48

SOLVING WORD PROBLEMS FOR LIFE
Day 79

Name _____ Date _____

Chuck had to read a book that was 434 pages in length. If he had to read it in 2 weeks, how many pages a day must he read?

HOW DO YOU SOLVE IT?

SOLVING WORD PROBLEMS FOR LIFE
Day 80—Quiz 5

Name _____ Date _____

Solve the following word problems. Show your work!

1. The landscaping crew planted 8 rows with 25 tulips in each row. How many tulips did they plant?

2. How many calories did Josh consume if he ate a biscuit with sausage and egg (529 calories), a raspberry Danish (414 calories), and milk (125 calories)?

3. Chuck had to read a book with 434 pages in 2 weeks. How many pages must he read each day?

4. How much did Antonio spend if he bought a shirt for $25.00, jeans for $42.50, and a belt for $18.00?

5. What is the visual cue for multiplying?

49

Unit 6

Day 81 – Day 96

SOLVING WORD PROBLEMS FOR LIFE
Day 81

Name _____ Date _____

Gabe's basketball coach wanted him to practice 225 free throws a day. If he shot 139 free throws before dinner, how many more free throws does he need to shoot after dinner?

HOW DO YOU SOLVE IT?

SOLVING WORD PROBLEMS FOR LIFE
Day 82

Name _____ Date _____

Toby and his girlfriend went to a movie. It started at 2:35 P.M. and ended at 5:03 P.M. How long was the movie?

HOW DO YOU SOLVE IT?

SOLVING WORD PROBLEMS FOR LIFE
Day 83

Name _____ Date _____

Tracy had 983 beads that she used to make necklaces. She organizes those beads into boxes that hold 40 beads each. How many boxes does she need?

HOW DO YOU SOLVE IT?

SOLVING WORD PROBLEMS FOR LIFE
Day 84

Name _____ Date _____

The weather forecaster stated that the record high for this day was 102°F and the record low was 78°F. What is the difference between the 2 record temperatures?

HOW DO YOU SOLVE IT?

SOLVING WORD PROBLEMS FOR LIFE
Day 86

Name _____ Date _____

Chip's dad grilled hamburgers for Chip and his friends. A total of 15 people ate half-pound hamburgers each. How much meat did he need?

HOW DO YOU SOLVE IT?

SOLVING WORD PROBLEMS FOR LIFE
Day 85

Name _____ Date _____

Ray's mom gave him 12 quarters and 3 $1 bills. How many 50¢ video games can he play?

HOW DO YOU SOLVE IT?

SOLVING WORD PROBLEMS FOR LIFE
Day 87

Name _____ Date _____

Seth and his uncle built a brick pathway to the flower garden. If it is 8 feet wide and 26 feet long, what is the area of the pathway?

HOW DO YOU SOLVE IT?

SOLVING WORD PROBLEMS FOR LIFE
Day 88

Name _____ Date _____

Danette's grandmother took her heart medicine every 8 hours and her pain medicine every 6 hours. If she took her first doses at 7:00 A.M., what are the next 2 times she will take her medicines?

HOW DO YOU SOLVE IT?

SOLVING WORD PROBLEMS FOR LIFE
Day 89

Name _____ Date _____

Davis sold 23 rolls of wrapping paper for $8 per roll and 17 rolls for $7 per roll for a school fundraiser. How much money did he raise?

HOW DO YOU SOLVE IT?

SOLVING WORD PROBLEMS FOR LIFE
Day 90

Name _____ Date _____

Dana's dad is a truck driver. He delivered 136 gallons of milk, 84 cartons of orange juice, 397 blocks of cheese, and 84 cartons of eggs to the grocery store. How many items did he deliver?

HOW DO YOU SOLVE IT?

SOLVING WORD PROBLEMS FOR LIFE
Day 91

Name _____ Date _____

There are 52 cards in a deck of cards. Of those, 12 are face cards. What fraction are the remaining cards?

HOW DO YOU SOLVE IT?

Set up as a fraction and reduce to the lowest terms.

SOLVING WORD PROBLEMS FOR LIFE
Day 92

Name _____ Date _____

Virginia gets $6 per week for her allowance. $1 is for church, $2 are for savings, and $3 are for spending money. If she wants to buy a portable DVD player for $213, how many weeks of her allowance will it take to buy it?

HOW DO YOU SOLVE IT?

SOLVING WORD PROBLEMS FOR LIFE
Day 93

Name _____ Date _____

Jerry and his brother were putting a 1,000-piece puzzle together. If 483 pieces had been put together, how many pieces were left?

HOW DO YOU SOLVE IT?

SOLVING WORD PROBLEMS FOR LIFE
Day 94

Name _____ Date _____

Today is July 7. Shelley's birthday is on September 1. How many more days until her birthday?

HOW DO YOU SOLVE IT?

Use a calendar to count the days.

SOLVING WORD PROBLEMS FOR LIFE
Day 95

Name _____ Date _____

4 laps on a track equal 1 mile. If Kim ran 25 laps, how many miles did she run?

HOW DO YOU SOLVE IT?

SOLVING WORD PROBLEMS FOR LIFE
Day 96—Quiz 6

Name _____ Date _____

Solve the following word problems. Show your work!

1. Seth and his uncle built a brick pathway that was 8 feet wide and 26 feet long. What is the area of the pathway?

2. Jerry and his brother put a 1,000-piece puzzle together. If 483 pieces had been put together, how many pieces were left?

3. Why is the saw the visual cue for dividing?

4. Dana's dad delivered 136 gallons of milk, 84 cartons of orange juice, 397 blocks of cheese, and 84 cartons of eggs. How many items did he deliver?

5. 4 laps on a track equal 1 mile. If Kim ran 25 laps, how many miles did she run?

Unit 7

Day 97–Day 112

SOLVING WORD PROBLEMS FOR LIFE
Day 97

Name _____ Date _____

Ashton opened a savings account with $50. He put in another $35 that he received as birthday gifts. At Christmas, he put in $75 from family gifts. How much money does he have in his savings account?

HOW DO YOU SOLVE IT?

SOLVING WORD PROBLEMS FOR LIFE
Day 98

Name _____ Date _____

Mel's family took 6 rolls of pictures while on their vacation. 3 rolls had 24 pictures per roll. 3 rolls had 36 pictures per roll. How many pictures did they take?

HOW DO YOU SOLVE IT?

SOLVING WORD PROBLEMS FOR LIFE
Day 99

Name _____ Date _____

Sheila lives one-third (or 0.33) of a mile from school, so she rides her bike to and from there every day. How many miles does she ride during a 5-day school week?

HOW DO YOU SOLVE IT?

SOLVING WORD PROBLEMS FOR LIFE
Day 100

Name _____ Date _____

6 people each had some candy. Each person kept 1 piece and gave 2 pieces away. How many pieces of candy were there?

HOW DO YOU SOLVE IT?

Draw a chart to solve:

SOLVING WORD PROBLEMS FOR LIFE
Day 101

Name _____   Date _____

Ernesto's teacher gave him a container full of 240 new pencils. One-sixth of the pencils were red, one-half were green, and one-third were blue. How many pencils of each color were there?

HOW DO YOU SOLVE IT?

SOLVING WORD PROBLEMS FOR LIFE
Day 102

Name _____   Date _____

Vanessa's older sister worked 34 hours one week, 20 hours the next week, 26 hours the next week, and 18 hours the last week of the month. How many hours did she work this month?

HOW DO YOU SOLVE IT?

SOLVING WORD PROBLEMS FOR LIFE
Day 103

Name _____ Date _____

The skid marks on the road from the wreck measured 250 yards. The officer's report required that it be written in feet. How many feet is that?

HOW DO YOU SOLVE IT?

SOLVING WORD PROBLEMS FOR LIFE
Day 104

Name _____ Date _____

The game board has 95 spaces to land on when you roll the dice. If Warren rolled a double 6 four times in a row, how many more spaces would he have to move past to win the game?

HOW DO YOU SOLVE IT?

SOLVING WORD PROBLEMS FOR LIFE
Day 105

Name _____ Date _____

The boiling point of water is 212°F, and the freezing point is 32°F. What is the difference between these 2 temperatures?

HOW DO YOU SOLVE IT?

SOLVING WORD PROBLEMS FOR LIFE
Day 106

Name _____ Date _____

10,512 tickets were sold for the 1st night of the concert. 12,350 tickets were sold for the 2nd night. How many more tickets were sold for the 2nd night of the concert?

HOW DO YOU SOLVE IT?

SOLVING WORD PROBLEMS FOR LIFE
Day 107

Name _____ Date _____

The cheerleading team held a carwash to raise money for camp. If they charged $7 per vehicle, how many vehicles would they need to wash to raise $310?

HOW DO YOU SOLVE IT?

SOLVING WORD PROBLEMS FOR LIFE
Day 108

Name _____ Date _____

Pedro was training for a marathon. He ran 10.5 miles on Monday, 6.75 miles on Tuesday, 18 miles on Wednesday, 13.25 miles on Friday, and 23.5 miles on Sunday. How many miles did he run?

HOW DO YOU SOLVE IT?

SOLVING WORD PROBLEMS FOR LIFE
Day 109

Name _____ Date _____

Dennis' family went on a missionary trip for 42 months. How many years is that?

HOW DO YOU SOLVE IT?

SOLVING WORD PROBLEMS FOR LIFE
Day 110

Name _____ Date _____

The pizza store owner wanted the cooks to put 7 pieces of pepperoni on each slice of pizza. How many pepperonis would be put on 5 pizzas that were 8 slices each?

HOW DO YOU SOLVE IT?

SOLVING WORD PROBLEMS FOR LIFE
Day 111

Name _____ Date _____

Yolanda spent $6.50 for a movie ticket. She bought a box of popcorn for $3.75 and a drink for $2.00. How much money did she spend at the movies?

HOW DO YOU SOLVE IT?

SOLVING WORD PROBLEMS FOR LIFE
Day 112—Quiz 7

Name _____ Date _____

Solve the following word problems. Show your work!

1. The boiling point of water is 212°F, and the freezing point is 32°F. What is the difference between these 2 temperatures?

2. If the cooks had to put 7 pieces of pepperoni on each slice of pizza, how many pepperonis would be on 5 pizzas with 8 slices each?

3. Ashton's savings account was opened with $50. He put in $35 after his birthday and $75 after Christmas. How much money does he have in his savings account?

4. When you solve for area, what 2 visual cues would you use?

5. The skid marks from the wreck measured 250 yards. How many feet would that be?

Unit 8

Day 113 – Day 128

SOLVING WORD PROBLEMS FOR LIFE
Day 113

Name _____ Date _____

The hardware store sold 37 wrenches, 110 hammers, 95 screwdrivers, 76 saws, and 25 pliers this week. How many tools were sold?

HOW DO YOU SOLVE IT?

SOLVING WORD PROBLEMS FOR LIFE
Day 114

Name _____ Date _____

A bakery baked 12 dozen cookies to sell. If 78 cookies were bought, how many cookies were left?

HOW DO YOU SOLVE IT?

72

SOLVING WORD PROBLEMS FOR LIFE
Day 115

Name _____ Date _____

Valerie's mom told her that she could play at her best friend's house for 3 1/2 hours. If it was 1:15 P.M. when she left, what time does she need to be home?

HOW DO YOU SOLVE IT?

SOLVING WORD PROBLEMS FOR LIFE
Day 116

Name _____ Date _____

Hasan's dad brought a package of chocolate candies to the park. If there are 150 pieces in the package, how many pieces of candy will each of the 9 children get to eat for a snack? How many pieces are left over for Hasan's dad to eat?

HOW DO YOU SOLVE IT?

73

SOLVING WORD PROBLEMS FOR LIFE
Day 117

Name _____ Date _____

A clown had 220 balloons to sell at the fair throughout the day. 37 balloons blew away. 119 balloons were sold. How many balloons did he have left?

HOW DO YOU SOLVE IT?

SOLVING WORD PROBLEMS FOR LIFE
Day 118

Name _____ Date _____

Duncan counted the ceiling tiles in the lunchroom during detention. The lunchroom was 26 tiles long and 15 tiles wide. If 12 tiles were missing, how many tiles were there?

HOW DO YOU SOLVE IT?

SOLVING WORD PROBLEMS FOR LIFE
Day 119

Name _____ Date _____

Rasheed's mom had "Buy one, get one free" coupons. They ordered 2 meals that cost $10.99 each and 2 meals that cost $13.50 each. How much did dinner cost?

HOW DO YOU SOLVE IT?

SOLVING WORD PROBLEMS FOR LIFE
Day 120

Name _____ Date _____

Drew is 6'7" tall. How many total inches is he?

HOW DO YOU SOLVE IT?

SOLVING WORD PROBLEMS FOR LIFE
Day 121

Name _____ Date _____

Sherry's family drove to her Uncle John's house for a visit. They drove 370 miles before eating lunch. Then, they drove 139 miles before a restroom break. Finally, after another 46 miles, they arrived at his house. How many miles did they travel?

HOW DO YOU SOLVE IT?

SOLVING WORD PROBLEMS FOR LIFE
Day 122

Name _____ Date _____

The grocery store had a sale on canned vegetables: 3 cans for $1.50. If Isabelle spent $45.00, how many cans of vegetables did she buy?

HOW DO YOU SOLVE IT?

SOLVING WORD PROBLEMS FOR LIFE
Day 123

Name _____ Date _____

Tony, the carpenter, was completing the deck work on his new house. It took 144 pieces of wood to floor the deck. If he used 6 nails on each piece, how many nails did he use?

HOW DO YOU SOLVE IT?

SOLVING WORD PROBLEMS FOR LIFE
Day 124

Name _____ Date _____

Carlos catches the school bus at 6:58 A.M. He takes 12 minutes to take a shower, 15 minutes to get ready, and 20 minutes to eat breakfast. At what time does he need to get up?

HOW DO YOU SOLVE IT?

SOLVING WORD PROBLEMS FOR LIFE
Day 125

Name _____ Date _____

Candice's checkbook balance was $325.67. She spent $42.39 at the grocery store, $31.75 for a new blouse, and $27.40 for a birthday gift. What is her balance now?

HOW DO YOU SOLVE IT?

SOLVING WORD PROBLEMS FOR LIFE
Day 126

Name _____ Date _____

Joseph found a wallet with 3 $50 bills, 10 $20 bills, 7 $10 bills, and 16 $1 bills. How much money was in the lost wallet?

HOW DO YOU SOLVE IT?

SOLVING WORD PROBLEMS FOR LIFE
Day 127

Name _____ Date _____

Morgan bought some land for a farm. He wanted to build a rectangular fence. The pasture was 150 yards long and 75 yards wide. How much fencing did he need to buy?

HOW DO YOU SOLVE IT?

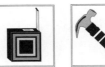

SOLVING WORD PROBLEMS FOR LIFE
Day 128—Quiz 8

Name _____ Date _____

Solve the following word problems. Show your work!

1. Duncan counted the tiles in the lunchroom. It was 26 tiles long and 15 tiles wide. If 12 tiles were missing, how many tiles were there?

2. Candice's checkbook balance was $325.67. She spent $42.39 at the grocery store, $31.75 for a new blouse, and $27.40 for a new blouse. What is her new balance?

3. If a problem wanted you to multiply and then subtract, what 2 visual cues would you use?

4. The hardware store sold 37 wrenches, 110 hammers, 95 screwdrivers, 76 saws, and 25 pliers this week. How many tools were sold?

5. Hasan's dad shared a package of 150 chocolate candies at the park. If there were 9 children, how many pieces did each child get? How many pieces were left over for Hasan's dad?

Unit 9

Day 129–Day 144

SOLVING WORD PROBLEMS FOR LIFE
Day 129

Name _____ Date _____

For the family reunion at the lake house, the Fennells cooked hot dogs on the grill. There are 12 hot dogs in a package and 8 buns in a package. How many packages of each will they need if there are 50 people?

HOW DO YOU SOLVE IT?

SOLVING WORD PROBLEMS FOR LIFE
Day 130

Name _____ Date _____

A farmer had 30 goats. One-fifth of the goats slept during the day. One-half of them grazed on grass near the barn. One-sixth of them hid under the front porch. How many goats are unaccounted for?

HOW DO YOU SOLVE IT?

SOLVING WORD PROBLEMS FOR LIFE
Day 131

Name _____ Date _____

Nicole went to piano lessons twice a week for hour and a half sessions. Her parents wanted her to practice the piano 30 minutes per day on the days she did not have lessons. How many hours did she play in 4 weeks?

HOW DO YOU SOLVE IT?

SOLVING WORD PROBLEMS FOR LIFE
Day 132

Name _____ Date _____

Over the last 5 years, Dallas has climbed up Mt. Kilimanjaro (19,563 feet), Mt. Elbrus (18,481 feet), and Mt. Everest (29,035 feet). How many feet of steep mountain climbing has he completed?

HOW DO YOU SOLVE IT?

SOLVING WORD PROBLEMS FOR LIFE
Day 133

Name _____ Date _____

A. J. ran 5 miles today. If 1 mile equals 1,760 yards, how many yards did his run total?

HOW DO YOU SOLVE IT?

SOLVING WORD PROBLEMS FOR LIFE
Day 134

Name _____ Date _____

Mrs. Anderson had a grab bag for rewarding students' good behavior. There were 6 sparkle pencils, 4 keychains, 8 mini-games, and 2 ice cream coupons in the bag. What are the chances of choosing each item?

HOW DO YOU SOLVE IT?

Write the correct fractions and reduce them to the lowest terms.

SOLVING WORD PROBLEMS FOR LIFE
Day 135

Name _____ Date _____

A great white shark is 26 feet long, and a tiger shark is 216 inches long. What is the difference in their lengths? Give the answer in inches.

HOW DO YOU SOLVE IT?

SOLVING WORD PROBLEMS FOR LIFE
Day 136

Name _____ Date _____

Holly bought a terrarium for her hermit crabs. It measured 10 inches in length, 8 inches in width, and 6 inches in height. What is the volume of the terrarium?

HOW DO YOU SOLVE IT?

SOLVING WORD PROBLEMS FOR LIFE
Day 137

Name _____ Date _____

Chance's chore is to pick up toys every 3 days. This month and next month have 31 days each. If he starts on the first day of the first month, how many times will he pick up toys?

HOW DO YOU SOLVE IT?

Draw a chart.

SOLVING WORD PROBLEMS FOR LIFE
Day 138

Name _____ Date _____

Andre's plane leaves at 9:40 P.M. It takes him 45 minutes to get ready, 30 minutes to drive to the airport, and 30 minutes to get his luggage checked in and walk to the gate. What time does he need to get up?

HOW DO YOU SOLVE IT?

SOLVING WORD PROBLEMS FOR LIFE
Day 140

Name _____ Date _____

Amad's motorcycle holds 15 gallons of gas. If gas is $1.72 per gallon, how much will it cost to fill up the tank?

HOW DO YOU SOLVE IT?

SOLVING WORD PROBLEMS FOR LIFE
Day 139

Name _____ Date _____

The par 4 hole was 392 yards. Aimee's first shot was 125 yards. Her second shot was 103 yards. Her third shot was 131 yards. What does her fourth shot need to be for her to make par?

HOW DO YOU SOLVE IT?

SOLVING WORD PROBLEMS FOR LIFE
Day 141

Name _____ Date _____

Griffin's dad bought several 6-foot-long 2'×4' boards to build a tree house. If each board needed to be 18 inches long, how many pieces was each board cut into?

HOW DO YOU SOLVE IT?

SOLVING WORD PROBLEMS FOR LIFE
Day 142

Name _____ Date _____

Palmer had a summer job cutting grass. What was the total amount of money that he made if he made $55 in June, $110 in July, and $70 in August?

HOW DO YOU SOLVE IT?

SOLVING WORD PROBLEMS FOR LIFE
Day 143

Name _____ Date _____

An 18-wheeler truck had 3,278 pounds of cargo on it when it was weighed at the weighing station. If the weight limit was 2 tons, how much over or under was the cargo?

HOW DO YOU SOLVE IT?

SOLVING WORD PROBLEMS FOR LIFE
Day 144—Quiz 9

Name _____ Date _____

Solve the following word problems. Show your work!

1. Dallas climbed Mt. Kilimanjaro (19,563 feet), Mt. Elbrus (18,481 feet), and Mt. Everest (29,035 feet). How many feet of climbing did he accomplish?

2. If a problem deals with adding money, which 2 visual cues would you use?

3. The par 4 hole was 392 yards. Aimee's first shot was 125 yards, her second shot was 103 yards, and her third shot was 131 yards. How many yards must her fourth shot be to reach par?

4. Holly bought a terrarium for her hermit crabs that measured 10 inches by 8 inches by 6 inches. What is the volume of her terrarium?

5. A. J. ran 5 miles today. If 1 mile equals 1,760 yards, how many yards did he run?

Unit 10

Day 145–Day 160

SOLVING WORD PROBLEMS FOR LIFE
Day 145

Name _____ Date _____

George Washington, our first president, was born in 1732 and died in 1799. Ronald Reagan, our fortieth president, was born in 1911 and died in 2004. How old was each president when he died?

HOW DO YOU SOLVE IT?

SOLVING WORD PROBLEMS FOR LIFE
Day 146

Name _____ Date _____

Velvet's birthday party was at the movie theater. There were 12 girls at the party who each ate three-quarters of a tub of popcorn. How many tubs of popcorn did her mom buy?

HOW DO YOU SOLVE IT?

SOLVING WORD PROBLEMS FOR LIFE
Day 147

Name _____ Date _____

Today's temperature was 82°F. The record high for today was 100°F, and the record low was 57°F. What is the difference between today's temperature and the record high? the record low?

HOW DO YOU SOLVE IT?

SOLVING WORD PROBLEMS FOR LIFE
Day 148

Name _____ Date _____

Our favorite restaurant serves a "veggie special," which is three vegetables for $4.99, or they can be ordered for $1.75 each. What is the savings of the "special" rather than ordering the vegetables separately?

HOW DO YOU SOLVE IT?

SOLVING WORD PROBLEMS FOR LIFE
Day 150

Name _____ Date _____

On their hiking trip, the boys took turns carrying the tent. Kasim carried it 3 1/2 miles, Bryan carried it 2 3/4 miles, and Jarod carried it 4 1/4 miles. How many miles did they hike before they pitched their tent?

HOW DO YOU SOLVE IT?

SOLVING WORD PROBLEMS FOR LIFE
Day 149

Name _____ Date _____

Patton's dad gave him $15 to buy a vacation souvenir. He found a T-shirt that costs $12 plus 65¢ tax. How much change did he get back?

HOW DO YOU SOLVE IT?

SOLVING WORD PROBLEMS FOR LIFE
Day 151

Name _____ Date _____

The liquid laundry detergent container holds 300 fluid ounces. How many small loads could be washed with 1.5 fluid ounces of detergent? medium loads with 3 fluid ounces? large loads with 4.5 fluid ounces?

HOW DO YOU SOLVE IT?

SOLVING WORD PROBLEMS FOR LIFE
Day 152

Name _____ Date _____

The statue in the park is 25 1/2 feet tall. How many inches tall is it?

HOW DO YOU SOLVE IT?

SOLVING WORD PROBLEMS FOR LIFE
Day 153

Name _____ Date _____

Denise has completed three-quarters of her assignment, Timothy has completed 0.40 of his assignment, and Mechelle has completed 80% of her assignment. Draw a chart that illustrates who has completed the largest amount of the assignment.

SOLVING WORD PROBLEMS FOR LIFE
Day 154

Name _____ Date _____

In the year 2070, our country will be 294 years old. How many centuries, decades, and years would that be?

HOW DO YOU SOLVE IT?

SOLVING WORD PROBLEMS FOR LIFE
Day 156

Name _____ Date _____

The Smith family had 372 miles to drive to get to their cousin's house. They drove 118 miles before eating lunch. Then, they drove another 136 miles before needing a restroom break. How many more miles until they get there?

HOW DO YOU SOLVE IT?

SOLVING WORD PROBLEMS FOR LIFE
Day 155

Name _____ Date _____

Hannah's parents paid $1,395 for a down payment on her braces. They will be paying $160 per month for 20 months. How much will Hannah's braces cost?

HOW DO YOU SOLVE IT?

SOLVING WORD PROBLEMS FOR LIFE
Day 157

Name _____ Date _____

Timberlake Elementary School donated the following number of cans of food to the homeless shelter: kindergarten—716, 1st grade—599, 2nd grade—1,031, 3rd grade—480, 4th grade—922, and 5th grade—1,265. How many cans were donated?

HOW DO YOU SOLVE IT?

SOLVING WORD PROBLEMS FOR LIFE
Day 158

Name _____ Date _____

A family of 4 wants to go to a hockey game. Tickets are $38.00 each. Parking is $12.00. All of them want to eat a hot dog (costing $4.25 each) and a drink (costing $2.00 each) for dinner while at the game. How much will the family event cost?

HOW DO YOU SOLVE IT?

SOLVING WORD PROBLEMS FOR LIFE
Day 159

Name _____ Date _____

Shoe Express had a sale on shoes—two pairs for $70. Shoe Stop also had a sale—buy one pair and get the second pair half off. Which store was the better deal if one pair of shoes was $48 and the other pair was $40?

HOW DO YOU SOLVE IT?

SOLVING WORD PROBLEMS FOR LIFE
Day 160—Quiz 10

Name _____ Date _____

Solve the following word problems. Show your work!

1. Patton's dad gave him $15. He bought a T-shirt for $12 plus 65¢ tax. How much change did he get back?

2. A family of 4 wants to go to a hockey game. Tickets are $38.00 each. Parking is $12.00. Hot dogs are $4.25 each, and drinks are $2.00 each. How much will it cost for them to go to the hockey game and each have a hot dog and soda for dinner?

3. The Smith family had 372 miles to drive to their cousin's house. They drove 118 miles to lunch, and then 136 miles before needing a restroom break. How many more miles to go?

4. The statue in the park is 25 1/2 feet tall. How many inches tall is that?

5. Velvet's birthday party was at the movies. If 12 girls ate three-quarters of a tub of popcorn each, how many tubs of popcorn did her mom buy?

Day 161 – Day 180

SOLVING WORD PROBLEMS FOR LIFE
Day 161

Name _____ Date _____

A gallon of milk was in the refrigerator. Bubba drank 2 pints of milk and his cat drank 1 1/2 pints of milk. How many pints of milk were left in the gallon jug?

HOW DO YOU SOLVE IT?

SOLVING WORD PROBLEMS FOR LIFE
Day 162

Name _____ Date _____

Ms. Ingles gave this assignment for homework: Solve every third problem beginning at 1 and ending at 100. How many problems did the students have to work?

HOW DO YOU SOLVE IT?

Use a chart to solve.

SOLVING WORD PROBLEMS FOR LIFE
Day 164

Name _____ Date _____

Chad hiked on a trail for 4,100 feet. The next day, he hiked another 3,525 feet on the trail. On third day, he hiked the last 2,935 feet of the trail. If 1 mile equals 5,280 feet, how many miles did Chad hike?

HOW DO YOU SOLVE IT?

SOLVING WORD PROBLEMS FOR LIFE
Day 163

Name _____ Date _____

Coach Fitzgerald has his students sit in rows for roll call. There are 9 rows with 12 students in each row. If 16 students are absent today, how many students are present?

HOW DO YOU SOLVE IT?

103

SOLVING WORD PROBLEMS FOR LIFE
Day 165

Name _____ Date _____

Candice's mom gave her a budget of $75 for her birthday party. She spent $21 for the cake, $15 for the invitations and thank you notes, and $28 for the paper supplies. How much money does she have left?

HOW DO YOU SOLVE IT?

SOLVING WORD PROBLEMS FOR LIFE
Day 166

Name _____ Date _____

The Patel family had $2,369.20 in their checking account. The house payment was $873.95. The water bill was $40.08. The power bill was $110.71. The cable/Internet bill was $85.00. How much money did they have left in their checking account?

HOW DO YOU SOLVE IT?

Name _____ Date _____

At the basketball awards banquet, ice cream cups were given out for dessert. 12 ice cream cups were in each box. If there are 125 players and 225 parents there, how many boxes of ice cream cups were needed?

HOW DO YOU SOLVE IT?

Name _____ Date _____

The brick fence at the front of Samuel's neighborhood is 25 yards long and 3 yards high. What is the area of the fence in feet?

HOW DO YOU SOLVE IT?

SOLVING WORD PROBLEMS FOR LIFE
Day 169

Name _____ Date _____

Mr. Kell's class sold 250 containers of cookie dough. Derek sold one-tenth of the total, Connie sold one-fifth of the total, Shaquita sold three-fifths of the total; and Aimee sold one-tenth of the total. How many containers of cookie dough did each student sell?

HOW DO YOU SOLVE IT?

SOLVING WORD PROBLEMS FOR LIFE
Day 170

Name _____ Date _____

At Brianne's birthday party, the girls made bead necklaces. She bought 125 red beads, 300 black beads, 200 silver beads, 200 gold beads, and 175 clear beads. If each necklace holds 100 beads, how many necklaces could the girls make?

HOW DO YOU SOLVE IT?

The temperatures for this week were: Monday 82°F, Tuesday 79°F, Wednesday 85°F, Thursday 81°F, and Friday 77°F. What was the average temperature for this 5-day period?

HOW DO YOU SOLVE IT?

The airline gives frequent flyers a "free" coach seat ticket for every 10,000 miles flown. Chelsea's dad traveled 5,732 miles this year. How many more miles must he travel before he is eligible for a free ticket?

HOW DO YOU SOLVE IT?

SOLVING WORD PROBLEMS FOR LIFE
Day 173

Name _____ Date _____

Terri left her house at 10:20 A.M. She spent 2 hours and 15 minutes at her friends' house. She spent 1 hour and 30 minutes at the library. She spent 40 minutes at the park. What time will it be at the end of those activities?

HOW DO YOU SOLVE IT?

SOLVING WORD PROBLEMS FOR LIFE
Day 174

Name _____ Date _____

The Blackhawks scored 33 two-point baskets and 7 three-point baskets. What is their score?

HOW DO YOU SOLVE IT?

SOLVING WORD PROBLEMS FOR LIFE
Day 175

Name _____ Date _____

Eden wanted to buy a $128 pair of shoes. The shoes were on sale for 20% off. What was the new price?

HOW DO YOU SOLVE IT?

SOLVING WORD PROBLEMS FOR LIFE
Day 176—Quiz 11

Name _____ Date _____

Solve the following word problems. Show your work!

1. Coach Fitzgerald has the students sit in 9 rows with 12 students in each row for roll call. If 16 students are absent, how many students are present?

2. The brick fence was 25 yards long and 3 yards high. What is the area of the fence in yards?

3. Eden bought a $128 pair of shoes. The sale was 20% off. What is the new price with the sale?

4. Candice's mom gave her a budget of $75 for her party. She spent $21 for the cake, $15 for the invitations and thank you notes, and $28 for the paper supplies. How much money did she have left?

5. Terri left her house at 10:20 A.M. She spent 2 hours and 15 minutes at her friends' house, 1 hour and 30 minutes at the library, and 40 minutes at the park. What time will it be at the end of those activities?

SOLVING WORD PROBLEMS FOR LIFE
Day 177

Name _____ Date _____

YOUR WORD PROBLEM ABILITIES 1

Directions: Complete the following chart. Circle the box that best represents your feeling for each statement.

1. I feel that my problem-solving skills were weak before starting the daily word problems.	You bet! I didn't have a clue!	I don't know. I'm not sure what my abilities were.	No way! I could solve them on my own.
2. The visual cues helped me know how to solve the problem.	They were very helpful!	They confused me more than they helped me.	I didn't need them!
3. I saw growth in being able to set up and solve word problems.	I was amazed at how much I grew!	I guess I saw some growth, but I still don't feel confident.	I wasn't paying attention to my growth.
4. I thought the problems were challenging.	I liked the challenge!	It frustrated me at times, but I solved some of them.	I don't like challenges—they're too hard!
5. I feel much stronger in my problem-solving skills.	Yes! I can solve lots of word problems.	Somewhat stronger. I still need help.	No. I didn't get much from doing the problems.

SOLVING WORD PROBLEMS FOR LIFE
Day 178

Name _____ Date _____

YOUR WORD PROBLEM ABILITIES 2

Directions: Match each visual cue to its explanation.

1.

2.

3.

4.

5.

6.

A. To multiply your efforts in moving something

B. To measure the distance or length of something

C. To put something more with your existing project

D. To know how to solve for time, temperature, and money

E. To cut something into smaller pieces

F. To take out or remove

YOUR WORD PROBLEM ABILITIES 3

Directions: Explain the *visual* cues/steps needed to solve the problem, and give the answer to each problem.

1. Two boys wanted to swap collector's baseball cards. Chip had 2 cards that were each worth $5.60. Mitchell had 3 cards that were each worth $3.05. Was it an even trade? If not, what was the difference in money value?

2. There are 30 days in the month of June. The first day of the month started on a Monday. Alexandria went to Tae Kwon Do practice every Tuesday and Thursday. How many times did she attend practice during June?

SOLVING WORD PROBLEMS FOR LIFE
Day 180

Name _____ Date _____

**Last day of school!
Celebrate! Free day!
You earned it!**

111

Hard Hat Thinking 1–5

Hard Hat Thinking 1

Name _____ Date _____

Directions: Solve the word problems. Show your work.

1. The Olympus Mons, a volcano on the planet Mars, is 79,000 feet in height. Mount Everest is 29,028 feet in height. What is the difference in their heights?

2. Julia's mom bought 24 rolls of toilet paper for $8.99 at the warehouse store. How much was each roll of toilet paper?

3. About 11 people in every 100 people are left-handed. If there are 5,200 people in a city, how many are left-handed?

4. A large sports equipment store donated these pieces of equipment to Central School District: 3,500 basketballs, 2,050 baseballs, 2,700 dodge balls, and 1,890 hula hoops. How many pieces of equipment were donated?

5. The fire department and police department had a celebration for all their families. 100 pizzas were ordered, but only three-quarters of the pizza ordered was eaten. How many pizzas were not eaten?

Hard Hat Thinking 2

Name _____ Date _____

Directions: Solve the word problems. Show your work.

1. Mrs. Birindelli needs to figure out how much tea she needs to make for the church luncheon. If each cup holds 8 ounces, how many gallons of tea would be needed for 220 people?

2. The library bought 250 fiction books, 150 nonfiction books, and 100 biographies this year. What fraction of the books were fiction? nonfiction? biographies? (Reduce to the lowest terms.)

3. Joann bought a home game system for $119.99. The 2 controllers were $32.95 each. The store gave a 15% discount when the game system and 2 controllers were purchased at the same time. What was the total cost with a 6% sales tax?

4. Daniel's family bought a new car that costs $24,500 with 0% financing. What would be the monthly payments if they financed it for 4 years? 5 years?

5. The gas price went from $1.69 per gallon to $2.10 per gallon. How much more money will it cost to fill up a 25-gallon tank?

Hard Hat Thinking 3

Name _____ Date _____

Directions: Solve the word problems. Show your work.

1. A gorilla was fed 12 pounds of bananas a day. How many pounds of bananas did the gorilla eat during the summer (June, July, and August)?

2. A professional basketball player had 1,013 attempts at field goals and made 750 of those attempts during his career. What percentage of the field goals did he make?

3. The Earth adds 2,000 pounds of weight per hour due to a constant shower of dust from outer space. How many pounds of weight are added to the Earth each year?

4. The brain makes up about one-fiftieth of a person's total body weight. If Grayson weighs 210 pounds, how much does his brain weigh?

5. A bank charges a monthly checking fee of $9.95 if the checking account balance goes below $100 and no charge if the balance remains above $100. The Wright family's account was above $100 for six months of the year. How much did they pay in fees this year?

Hard Hat Thinking 4

Name _____ Date _____

Directions: Solve the word problems. Show your work.

1. A landscaper wanted to design a flower bed with a 3'×3' fountain in the middle. The length of the flower bed was 12 feet, and the width was 9 feet. What was the actual area that could be used to plant flowers?

2. A sphinx moth's wings beat 30 times per second. How many times would the wings beat in 30 minutes?

3. It costs $1.25 to wash and $1.50 to dry a load of clothes at the laundromat. Treyton had 6 loads of laundry. How much money did he spend at the laundromat?

4. D'Andre had a backache. If he took pain medication every 8 hours for 2 days, how many times did he take his medicine?

5. Dylan and Gwen ate a wonderful dinner together. The total bill was $57.60. What would they leave for a tip if they tipped the server 15%? 20%?

Hard Hat Thinking 5

Name _____ Date _____

Directions: Solve the word problems. Show your work.

1. Dallas created a chain letter by sending it to 5 of his friends. It instructed them to copy it and send it to 5 more people. 4 out of 5 of his friends participated. How many letters were sent?

2. Cody needs 45 minutes to get ready. He needs 10 minutes to iron his work clothes. He needs 30 minutes to eat. If it is 3:00 P.M. and he needs to be to work by 5:30 P.M., how much spare time does he have?

3. Miguel is taken to another planet by aliens. On their planet, 1 year equals 12 Earth years. If he stays there 3 years, how old will he be when he returns if he was 10 years old when he left?

4. Tricia's mom gave her $200 to spend on clothes. A pair of jeans costs $37.50, a jacket costs $125, a sweater costs $45, and a shirt costs $35. Which 3 items could she buy and stay within her budget?

5. Jaime's grandparents saved their spare change for her college fund. When they gave it to her there were 105 nickels, 36 quarters, 270 dimes, and 637 pennies. How much money did they give her?

Units 1–11 Answer Key

Day 7

8 letters × 3 stamps each = 24 stamps

Day 8
Measuring Perimeter

25 yards + 25 yards + 14 yards + 14 yards = 78 yards

Day 9
Time

12:50 P.M. − 12:30 P.M. = 20 minutes of recess

Day 10

20 sunny days − 9 rainy days = 11 more sunny days

Day 11

69 single scoops + 54 double scoops = 123 cones of ice cream

Day 12
Money

$5.00 − $3.12 = $1.88

Day 13

4 rows × 6 tulips per row = 24 tulips

Day 14
Temperature

76°F − 43°F = 33°F

Day 15

39 tiger eyes + 26 jaspers + 10 chinas = 75 marbles

Day 16—Quiz 1

1. $1.88
2. 24 stamps
3. A screwdriver
4. 123
5. 20 minutes

Day 17

64 crayons − 18 crayons = 46 crayons left

Day 18

516 cars + 104 trucks + 791 SUVs + 28 motorcycles = 1,439 vehicles

Day 19
Money

$2.00 − $1.57 = $0.43   4 dimes and 3 pennies

Day 20
Measuring Area

9 inches × 9 inches = 81 inches^2

Day 21
Time

10:33 A.M. − 10:17 A.M. = 16 minutes

Day 22

Chandler   Mike

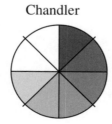
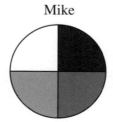

They ate the same amount: 6/8 = 3/4.

Day 23

6 girls × 7 laps each = 42 laps

Day 24

103 breakfasts + 347 lunches + 459 dinners = 909 meals

Day 25
Measuring Height

4 feet, 4 inches − 3 feet, 11 inches   (Must borrow 12 inches from the 4 feet—add the 12 inches to the 4 inches to get 16 inches.) = 5 inches of growth

Day 26
Money

7 cups × 5¢ = 35¢
2 quarters = 50¢ − 35¢ = 15¢ change

Day 27
Time

10:45 A.M. + 7 hours = 5:45 P.M. + 15 minutes = 7 hours, 15 minutes of sleep

Day 28

25 problems + 25 problems + 10 problems of extra credit = 60 problems

Day 29

27 pigs − 13 pigs in the mud = 14 pigs − 5 pigs eating = 9 pigs left at the barn

Day 30

7 weeks × 7 days/week = 49 days

Day 31

 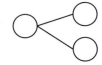

There are 9 girls with the new frog toys.

Day 32—Quiz 2

1. You are measuring the distance or length of something.
2. 42 laps
3. 9 pigs left
4. 43¢
5. 909 meals

Day 33
Money

$5.00 + 10 quarters ($2.50) + 6 nickels ($0.30) = $7.80

No, he doesn't have enough money.

Day 34

17 kids + 9 kids + 22 kids = 48 kids

Day 35

$135 − $58 = $77 more needed

Day 36
Time

6:23 P.M. − 5:05 P.M. = 1 hour, 18 minutes

Day 37

5 rows × 4 students/row = 20 students

Day 38
Temperature

152°F − 68°F = 84°F

Day 39

565 passengers − 379 passengers got off = 186 passengers left

Day 40

540 aluminum cans + 173 plastic bottles + 388 milk jugs = 1,101 items

Day 41
Money

$4.50 teddy bear + $1.25 card + $0.29 tax = $6.04
$10.00 − $6.04 = $3.96

Day 42

8 tentacles × 7 octopi = 56 octopus tentacles

Day 43
Measuring Perimeter

2.5 miles + 2.5 miles + 0.6 miles + 0.6 miles = 6.2 miles

Day 44
Time

7:30 A.M.+4 hours, 18 minutes=11:48 A.M.+2 hours, 12 minutes=2:00 P.M.

Day 45

Decade=10 years   10+10+10+6=36 years old

Day 46

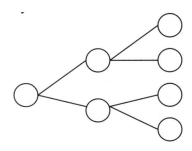   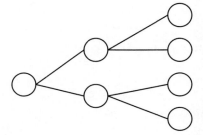

14 got chicken pox.

Day 47

320 pounds−17 pounds−17 pounds−17 pounds−17 pounds−8 pounds−6 pounds=238 pounds

Day 48—Quiz 3

1. 20 students
2. 48 kids
3. 186 passengers
4. 6.2 miles
5. They are used every day like goggles are used every time you use tools.

Day 49

73 boxes of doughnuts×12 doughnuts/dozen=876 doughnuts

Day 50
Money

$16.50+$35.75=$52.25

Day 51

720 gumballs×1/8 (red)=90 gumballs   720 gumballs×1/2 (yellow)=360 gumballs
720 gumballs×1/4 (blue)=180 gumballs   720 gumballs× 1/8 (green)=90 gumballs

Day 52

81 butterflies÷9 types of butterflies=9 butterflies of each type

Day 53

9,000 pieces of construction paper $-$ 6,395 pieces used $=$ 2,605 pieces left

Day 54
Time

23 minutes, 11 seconds $+$ 14 minutes, 57 seconds $+$ 9 minutes, 31 seconds $=$ 46 minutes, 99 seconds or 47 minutes, 39 seconds

Day 55
Measuring Area

24 inches wide $\times$ 40 inches long $=$ 960 inches^2

Day 56

8 packs of gum $\times$ 15 pieces/pack $=$ 120 pieces of gum

Day 57

12 $+$ 6 $+$ 12 $+$ 10 $+$ 20 $=$ 60 water balloons
12/60 $=$ 1/5 chance of orange   6/60 $=$ 1/10 chance of green
12/60 $=$ 1/5 chance of yellow   10/60 $=$ 1/6 chance of red
20/60 $=$ 1/3 chance of blue

Day 58
Money

$10.00 $-$ $9.24 $=$ $0.76   3 quarters and 1 penny

Day 59

6 $+$ 9 $+$ 13 $+$ 12 $+$ 7 $+$ 5 $+$ 10 $+$ 4 $=$ 66 animals

Day 60

65 kids invited $\div$ 8 kids/table $=$ 8 tables and 1 kid, so her parents will need 9 tables

Day 61

$75.00 $-$ $39.99 (ticket) $-$ $18.68 (lunch) $-$ $23.00 (souvenir) $=$ $-$$6.67, or $6.67 over his spending money

Day 62
Measurement

42 inches $\div$ 12 inches/foot $=$ 3 feet, 6 inches   4 feet is longer than 42 inches

Day 63
Time

24 hours/day × 3 days = 72 hours

Day 64—Quiz 4

1. You are adding to an existing project.
2. $52.25
3. 9 tables
4. 876 doughnuts
5. 960 inches^2

Day 65
Temperature

103.7°F − 98.5°F = 5.2°F

Day 66

2 + 4 + 6 + 8 + 10 + 12 + 14 + 16 + 18 + 20 + 22 + 24 + 26 + 28 + 30 + 32 + 34 + 36 + 38 + 40 + 42 + 44 + 46 + 48 + 50 + 52 + 54 + 56 + 58 + 60 + 62 + 64 + 66 + 68 + 70 + 72 + 74 = 1,406

Day 67

8 rows × 25 tulips/row = 200 tulips

Day 68
Measuring Volume

10 inches long × 4 inches wide × 6 inches high = 240 inches^3

Day 69
Money

$25.99 + $42.50 + $18.00 = $86.49

Day 70

2 eggs, 1 c. oil, 1 c. sugar, 2 c. flour, 1/2 tsp. baking soda, 1/4 tsp. salt, 1/2 tsp. cinnamon, 1/2 tsp. nutmeg, and 3 c. oatmeal

Day 71

2020 − 1998 = 22 years old

Day 72

1,500 boxes of cereal ÷ 5 shelves = 300 boxes of cereal/shelf

Day 73

$6+3+8+5+2=24$ items

6/24 or 1/4 chance of snakes   3/24 or 1/8 chance of rings

8/24 or 1/3 chance of books   5/24 chance of pencils

2/24 or 1/12 chance of animals

Day 74
Time

30 minutes (M)+30 minutes (T)+30 minutes (W)+30 minutes (Th)+30 minutes (F)+ 60 minutes (S)+60 minutes (Su)=270 minutes or 3 hours, 30 minutes

Day 75

152 fourth graders×6 doughnuts each=912 doughnuts

Day 76

529 calories (biscuit)+414 calories (Danish)+125 calories (milk)=1,068 calories

Day 77
Measuring Liquids

2 cups×8 pints/gallon=16 cups/gallon

16 cups/gallon×4 gallons=64 cups/gallon

Day 78

Holly=1/2×\$300=\$150   Matthew=1/6×\$300=\$50

Deirdre=1/3×\$300=\$100

Day 79

434 pages÷14 days/2 weeks=31 pages per day

Day 80

1. 200 tulips
2. 1,068 calories
3. 31 pages
4. \$86.49
5. Gears

Day 81

225−139=86 free throws

Day 82
Time

5:03 P.M. − 2:35 P.M. = 2 hours, 28 minutes

Day 83

983 beads ÷ 40 boxes = 24.5 boxes or 25 boxes

Day 84

102°F − 78°F = 24°F

Day 85
Money

25¢ + 25¢ + 25¢ + 25¢ + 25¢ + 25¢ + 25¢ + 25¢ + 25¢ + 25¢ + 25¢ + 25¢ + $1.00 + $1.00 + $1.00 = $6.00

$6.00 ÷ 50¢/game = 12 games

Day 86

1/2 pound hamburgers × 15 people = 15/2 or 7 1/2 pounds

Day 87
Measuring Area

8 feet wide × 26 feet long = 208 feet^2

Day 88
Medicine

Heart medicine   7:00 A.M. + 8 hours = 3:00 P.M. + 8 hours = 11:00 P.M.
Pain medicine   7:00 A.M. + 6 hours = 1:00 P.M. + 6 hours = 7:00 P.M.

Day 89

23 rolls × $8.00/roll = $184   17 rolls × $7.00/roll = $119
$184 + $119 = $303

Day 90

136 gallons of milk + 205 cartons of orange juice + 397 blocks of cheese + 84 cartons of eggs = 822 items

Day 91

52 cards − 12 face cards = 40 remaining cards
40/52 = 10/13

Day 92
Money

$213 ÷ $3 (spending money) = 71 weeks of allowance

Day 93

1,000 − 483 = 517 pieces of the puzzle left

Day 94

July has 31 days − 7 days (today's date) = 24 days; August has 31 days; 1 day of September
24 days + 31 days + 1 day = 56 days until her birthday

Day 95

25 laps ÷ 4 laps/mile = 6 1/4 miles

Day 96—Quiz 6

1. 208 feet^2
2. 517 pieces left
3. A saw divides or cuts something into pieces
4. 822 items
5. 6 1/4 miles

Day 97

$50 + $35 + $75 = $160

Day 98

24 pictures × 3 rolls = 72 pictures   36 pictures × 3 rolls = 108 pictures
72 + 108 = 180 pictures

Day 99

0.33 + 0.33 + 0.33 + 0.33 + 0.33 + 0.33 + 0.33 + 0.33 + 0.33 + 0.33 = 3.3 miles

Day 100

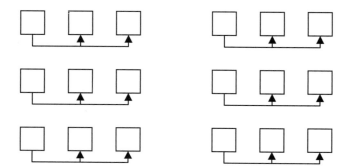

There were 18 pieces of candy.

Day 101

1/6×240 pencils=40 red pencils   1/2×240 pencils=120 green pencils
1/3×240 pencils=80 pencils

Day 102

34 hours+20 hours+26 hours+18 hours=98 hours

Day 103

250 yards÷3 feet/yard=83.33 feet

Day 104

12 (double 6)×4 rolls=48 spaces
95 total spaces−48 spaces=47 spaces left

Day 105

212°F−32°F=180°F

Day 106

12,350 tickets−10,512 tickets=1,838 more

Day 107

$310÷$7/vehicle=44.2 vehicles or 45 vehicles

Day 108

10.5 miles+6.75 miles+18 miles+13.25 miles+23.5 miles=72 miles

Day 109

42 months÷12 months/year=3 1/2 years

Day 110

7 pieces of pepperoni×8 slices=56 pepperonis×5 pizzas=280 pepperonis

Day 111

$6.50+$3.75+$2.00=$12.25

Day 112—Quiz 7

1. 180°F
2. 280 pepperonis
3. $160

4. Tape measure, gears

5. 83.33 feet

Day 113

$37 + 110 + 95 + 76 + 25 = 343$ tools

Day 114

12 cookies/dozen $\times 12 = 144$ cookies

$144 - 78 = 66$ cookies

Day 115

1:15 P.M. $+ 3$ hours $= 4:15$ P.M. $+ 30$ minutes $= 4:45$ P.M.

Day 116

150 pieces of candy $\div 9$ children $= 16$ pieces each and 6 pieces for Hasan's dad

Day 117

220 balloons $- 27$ blew away $= 183$ balloons $- 119$ sold $= 64$ balloons left

Day 118

26 tiles long $\times 15$ tiles wide $= 390$ tiles

390 tiles $- 12$ missing tiles $= 378$ tiles

Day 119

$10.99 + \$10.99$ (free) $+ \$13.50 + \$13.50$ (free) $= \$24.49$

Day 120

6 feet $\times 12$ inches/foot $= 72$ inches

72 inches $+ 7$ inches $= 79$ inches

Day 121

$370 + 139 + 46 = 555$ miles

Day 122

$45.00 \div \$1.50 = 30$ cans of vegetables

Day 123

144 pieces of wood $\times 6$ nails/piece $= 864$ nails

Day 124
Time

6:58 A.M. − 12 minutes = 6:46 A.M. − 15 minutes = 6:31 A.M. − 20 minutes = 6:11 A.M.

Day 125

$325.67 − $42.39 = $283.28 − $31.75 = $251.53 − $27.40 = $224.13

Day 126
Money

3 × $50 = $150   10 × $20 = $200   7 × $10 = $70   16 × $1 = $16
$150 + $200 + $70 + $16 = $436

Day 127
Measuring Perimeter

150 yds. + 150 yds. + 75 yds. + 75 yds. = 450 yds. of fencing

Day 128—Quiz 8

1. 378 tiles
2. $224.13
3. Gears, screwdriver
4. 343 tools
5. 16 pieces per child and 6 pieces for Hasan's dad

Day 129

50 people ÷ 12 hot dogs/package = 4.16 or 5 packages of hot dogs
50 people ÷ 8 buns/package = 6.25 or 7 packages of buns

Day 130

30 goats × 1/5 = 6 goats slept   30 goats × 1/2 = 15 goats grazing   30 goats × 1/6 = 5 goats hid
6 + 15 + 5 = 26 goats
30 total goats − 26 goats = 4 goats unattended

Day 131
Time

30 minutes = 1/2 hour
1 1/2 hr. + 1 1/2 hr. + 1/2 hr. + 1/2 hr. + 1/2 hr. + 1/2 hr. + 1/2 hr. = 5 1/2 hrs./week
5 1/2 hrs./week × 4 weeks = 22 hrs. of practice in 4 weeks

Day 132

19,563 ft. (Mt. Kilimanjaro) + 18,481 ft. (Mt. Elbrus) + 29,035 ft. (Mt. Everest) = 67,079 ft.

Day 133

1,760 yards/mile × 5 miles = 8,800 yards

Day 134

6 pencils + 4 keychains + 8 mini-games + 2 coupons = 20 items
6/20 pencils reduces to 3/10 chances of a pencil   4/20 keychains reduces to 1/5 chances of a keychain
8/20 mini-games reduces to 2/5 chances of a mini-game   2/20 coupons reduces to 1/10 chances of a coupon

Day 135

26 foot great white shark × 12 inches/foot = 312 inches
312 inches (great white shark) − 216 inches (tiger shark) = 96 inches difference

Day 136
Measuring Volume

10 inches × 8 inches × 6 inches = 480 inches³

Day 137

~~1~~ 2 3 ~~4~~ 5 6 ~~7~~ 8 9 ~~10~~ 11 12 ~~13~~ 14 15 ~~16~~ 17 18 ~~19~~ 20 21 ~~22~~ 23
24 ~~25~~ 26 27 ~~28~~ 29 30 ~~31~~ 1 2 ~~3~~ 4 5 ~~6~~ 7 8 ~~9~~ 10 11 ~~12~~ 13 14 ~~15~~
16 17 ~~18~~ 19 20 ~~21~~ 22 23 ~~24~~ 25 26 ~~27~~ 28 29 ~~30~~ 31
21 times

Day 138
Time

9:40 A.M. − 45 minutes = 8:55 A.M. − 30 minutes = 8:25 A.M. − 30 minutes = 7:55 A.M.

Day 139

125 yards + 103 yards + 131 yards = 359 yards
392 yards − 359 yards = 33 yards

Day 140

$1.72/gallon × 15 gallons = $25.80

Day 141

6 feet × 12 inches/foot = 72 inches
72 inches ÷ 18 inches/piece = 4 pieces

Day 142
Money

$55 (June) + $110 (July) + $70 (August) = $235

Day 143
Measuring weight

1 ton = 2,000 pounds
2 tons × 2,000 lbs./ton = 4,000 lbs.
4,000 lbs. − 3,278 lbs. = 722 lbs. under weight limit

Day 144—Quiz 9

1. 67,079 feet
2. Goggles, hammer
3. 33 yards
4. 480 inches^3
5. 8,800 yards

Day 145

George Washington   1799 − 1732 = 67 years old   Ronald Reagan   2004 − 1911 = 93 years old

Day 146

3/4 tub of popcorn × 12 girls = 9 tubs of popcorn to buy

Day 147
Temperature

100°F (record high) − 82°F = 18°F   82°F − 57°F (record low) = 25°F

Day 148

$1.75 × 3 vegetables = $5.25
$5.25 − $4.99 (cost of special) = $0.26 savings

Day 149
Money

$12.99 + $0.65 = $13.64
$15.00 − $13.64 = $1.36 in change

Day 150

3 1/2 miles (or 3 2/4 miles) + 2 3/4 miles + 4 1/4 miles = 9 6/4 or 9 + 1 1/2 = 10 1/2 miles

Day 151

small load − 300 fl. oz. ÷ 1.5 fl. oz. = 200 loads;   medium load − 300 fl. oz. ÷ 3 fl. oz. = 100 loads;
large load − 300 fl. oz. ÷ 4.5 fl. oz. = 66.67 loads

Day 152
Measuring Height

25 ft. × 12 in/ft. = 300 in.   1/2 ft. (or 6 in.)
300 in. + 6 in. = 306 in.

Day 153

Denise

Timothy

Mechelle

Mechelle has completed the largest amount of her assignment.

Day 154
Time

294 = 2 centuries (2 × 100 years), 9 decades (9 × 10 years), and 4 years

Day 155

$160/month × 20 months = $3,200
$3,200 + $1,395 (down payment) = $4,595

Day 156

372 miles − 118 miles (to lunch) = 254 miles − 136 miles (restroom break) = 118 miles to go

Day 157

716 cans (kindergarten) + 599 cans (1st grade) + 1,031 cans (2nd grade) + 480 cans (3rd grade) + 922 cans (4th grade) + 1,265 cans (5th grade) = 5,013 cans collected

Day 158
Money

$38 (ticket) × 4 = $152; $4.25 (hot dog) × 4 = $17; $2 (drink) × 4 = $8
$152 + $17 + $8 + $12 (parking) = $189

Day 159

Shoe Express = 2 pairs for $70
Shoe Stop = 1/2 price for second pair $40 ÷ 2 = $20
$48 + $20 = $68
Shoe Stop is the better deal.

Day 160—Quiz 10

1. $1.36
2. $189
3. 118 miles to go
4. 306 in.
5. 9 tubs of popcorn

Day 161

Measuring – 8 pints = 1 gallon
8 pints – 2 pints (Bubba) = 6 pints – 1 1/2 pints (cat) = 4 1/2 pints

Day 162

1 2 3 **4** 5 6 **7** 8 9 **10** 11 12 **13** 14 15 **16** 17 18 **19** 20
21 **22** 23 24 **25** 26 27 **28** 29 30 **31** 32 33 **34** 35 36 **37** 38
39 **40** 41 42 **43** 44 45 **46** 47 48 **49** 50 51 **52** 53 54 **55** 56
57 **58** 59 60 **61** 62 63 **64** 65 66 **67** 68 69 **70** 71 72 **73** 74
75 **76** 77 78 **79** 80 81 **82** 83 84 **85** 86 87 **88** 89 90 **91** 92
93 **94** 95 96 **97** 98 99 **100**

34 problems

Day 163

12 students/row × 9 rows = 108 students
108 students – 16 absent students = 92 students present

Day 164

4,100 feet + 3,525 feet + 2,935 feet = 10,560 feet
5,280 feet (1 mile) + 5,280 feet (1 mile) = 10,560 feet (2 miles)

Day 165

$75 – $21 (cake) = $54 – $15 (invitations and thank you notes) = $39 – $28 (paper supplies) = $11

Day 166
Money

$2,369.20 – $873.95 (house payment) = $1,495.25 – $40.08 (water bill) = $1,445.17 – $110.71 (power bill) = $1,344.46 – $85.00 (cable bill) = $1,259.46

Day 167

125 players + 225 parents = 350 people
350 people ÷ 12 ice cream cups/box = 29.16 or 30 boxes

Day 168
Measuring Area

25 yards (length) $\times$ 3 yards (height) = 75 yards^2
75 yards^2 $\times$ 3 feet/yard = 225 feet^2

Day 169

Derek   250 total containers $\times$ 1/10 = 25 containers
Connie   250 total containers $\times$ 1/5 = 50 containers
Shaquita   250 total containers $\times$ 3/5 = 150 containers
Aimee   250 total containers $\times$ 1/10 = 25 containers

Day 170

125 (red) + 300 (black) + 200 (silver) + 200 (gold) + 175 (clear) = 1,000 beads
1,000 beads $\div$ 100 beads/necklace = 10 necklaces

Day 171
Temperature

82°F + 79°F + 85°F + 81°F + 77°F = 404°F
404°F $\div$ 5 days = 80.8°F

Day 172

10,000 miles $-$ 5,732 miles = 4,268 more miles

Day 173
Time

10:20 A.M. + 2 hrs., 15 min. = 12:35 P.M. + 1 hr., 30 min. = 2:05 P.M. + 40 min. = 2:45 P.M.

Day 174

33 $\times$ 2-point baskets = 66 points   7 $\times$ 3-point baskets = 21 points
66 points + 21 points = 87 points

Day 175
Money

$128 $\times$ .20 = $25.60
$128 $-$ $25.50 (discount) = $101.50

Day 176—Quiz 11

1. 92 students
2. 75 yards^2
3. $101.50
4. $11
5. 2:45 P.M.

Day 177—Your Word Problem Abilities 1

Answers will vary.

Day 178—Your Word Problem Abilities 2

1. C   2. F   3. A   4. E   5. B   6. D

Day 179—Your Word Problem Abilities 3

1. Use goggles to represent money.
   Use gears for multiplying.
   Chip—2 cards × $5.60 = $11.20   Mitchell—3 cards × $3.05 = $9.15
   Use screwdriver for subtracting.
   $11.20 − $9.15 = $2.05
2. Draw chart of calendar for June.

S	M	T	W	T	F	S
	1	**2**	3	**4**	5	6
7	8	**9**	10	**11**	12	13
14	15	**16**	17	**18**	19	20
21	22	**23**	24	**25**	26	27
28	29	**30**				

There are 9 practice days in June.

Day 180—Free Day!

No answers.

Hard Hat Thinking Answer Key

Hard Hat Thinking 1

1. 79,000 feet − 29,028 feet = 49,972 feet
2. $8.99 ÷ 24 rolls of toilet paper = 37¢ per roll
3. 11/100 = ?/5,200   100 × 52 = 5200, so multiply 11 × 52. That equals 572 left-handed people out of 5,200 people.
4. 3,500 + 2,050 + 2,700 + 1,890 = 10,140 pieces of equipment
5. 100 pizza × 3/4 eaten = 75 eaten   100 total pizzas − 75 eaten = 25 pizzas not eaten

Hard Hat Thinking 2

1. 1 gallon = 128 ounces   128 ounces ÷ 8-ounce servings = 16 cups/gallon
   220 people ÷ 16 cups/gallon = 13.75 or 14 gallons needed
2. 250 fiction + 150 nonfiction + 100 biographies = 500 new books
   250/500 = 1/2 were fiction;   150/500 = 3/10 were nonfiction;   100/500 = 1/5 were biographies
3. $119.99 + $32.95 + $32.95 = $185.99 × 0.15 (discount) = $27.88 savings
   $185.99 − $27.88 = $158.11 (new price) × 0.06 (sales tax) = $9.49
   $158.11 + $9.49 = $167.60
4. $24,500 ÷ 48 months (4 years) = $510.42 $24,500 ÷ 60 months (5 years) = $408.34
5. $1.69 × 25 gallons = $42.25 $2.10 × 25 gallons = $52.50
   $52.50 − $42.25 = $10.25 more

Hard Hat Thinking 3

1. June = 30 days × 12 lbs./day = 360 lbs. of bananas   July = 31 days × 12 lbs./day = 372 lbs. of bananas   August = 31 days × 12 lbs./day = 372 lbs. of bananas
   360 + 372 + 372 = 1,104 lbs. of bananas
2. 750 field goals made ÷ 1,013 attempts at field goals = .740 or 74%
3. 2,000 lbs. of dust/hour × 24 hours/day = 48,000 lbs. of dust/day x 365 days/year = 17,520,000 lbs. of dust per year
4. 210 lbs . × 1/50 = 4.2 lbs.
5. $9.95/month × 6 months = $59.70 in checking fees

Hard Hat Thinking 4

1. 12 feet×9 feet=108 feet² (area of flower bed)   3 feet×3 feet=9 feet² (area of fountain)
   108 feet²−9 feet²=99 feet²
2. 30 times/second×60 seconds/minute=1,800 times/minute×30 minutes=54,000 times in 30 minutes
3. $1.25 (wash)×6 loads=$7.50 $1.50 (dry)×6 loads=$9.00
   $7.50+$9.00=$16.50
4. 24 hours=1 day   48 hours=2 days   48 hours÷taken every 8 hours=6 times
5. $57.60×0.15 tip=$8.64 $57.60×0.20 tip=$11.52

Hard Hat Thinking 5

1.

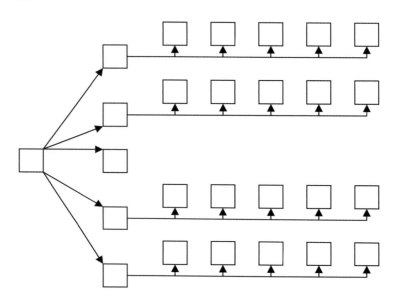

There were 26 chain letters sent.

2. 45 min. (get ready)+10 min. (iron clothes)+30 min. (eat)=85 minutes
   3:00 P.M.+85 minutes=4:25 P.M.   5:30 P.M.−4:25 P.M.=1 hour, 5 minutes spare time
3. 10 years old+12 years (1 year on that planet)+12 years (1 year on that planet)+12 years (1 year on
   that planet)=46 years old when he returns to Earth
4. $200.00 (spending money)−$37.50 (jeans)=$162.50−$125 (jacket)=$37.50−$35.00
   (shirt)=$2.50 left over
5. 105 nickels×0.05 (value of nickel)=$5.25   36 quarters×0.25 (value of quarter)=$9.00   270
   dimes×0.10 (value of dime)=$27.00   637×0.01 (value of penny)=$6.37 $5.25+$9+$27+
   $6.37=$47.62

Index

About the Author

Melony Brown, the founder of Construx Learning, taught special education for 11 years before writing full time for the last two years. She was inducted into Phi Lambda Theta and Phi Kappa Phi while pursuing her Master's degree. She is also a member of Phi Delta Kappa. Melony is married with two sons and resides in Smyrna, Georgia.